Call of the Deep
Diving Into God's Way of Life

Call of the Deep

Diving Into God's Way of Life

Linda Ray Miller

ABINGDON PRESS / *Nashville*

Call of the Deep: Diving Into God's Way of Life
by Linda Ray Miller

Copyright © 2007 by Abingdon Press

This book is printed on acid-free, elemental chlorine-free paper.

ISBN 978-0-687-64986-0

MANUFACTURED IN THE UNITED STATES OF AMERICA
07 08 09 10 11 12 13 14 15 16—10 9 8 7 6 5 4 3 2 1

Table of Contents

About the Writer

Linda Ray Miller, a native Texan, is a freelance writer residing in Nashville, Tennessee. She has served as a development editor for Children's Resources at The United Methodist Publishing House. An accomplished workshop leader, Linda Ray earned a masters degree in Religious Education from Perkins School of Theology at Southern Methodist University. She enjoys singing, gardening, working on her computer, theater, and keeping up with her two grown children.

A Word of Welcome

Call of the Deep: Diving Into God's Way of Life

Welcome to a five-session study of ways we can go deeper into God's Word and, in the process, become closer to God and to other people.

For a good part of my life, I lived on the Texas Gulf Coast. It was there I became acquainted with the ocean. Always being a little squeamish about stepping anywhere I could not see, I was content for a long time to play at the water's edge, where I would search for shells, watch the sea gulls, and revel in the smells and sounds of the ocean tides. As I became more comfortable, I was able to get out into the water and learn to float on the waves. I grew accustomed to the push and pull of the tide and learned to dive under oncoming waves to keep from being pushed back onto the shore. This was a totally new way to experience the ocean!

But I have been told that to truly experience the ocean, you need to put on scuba gear and really dive in. Underneath the surface, you can see strange sights that are impossible to see from the surface. You can learn of coral reefs, and stingrays, and be astounded at the fullness and diversity of God's universe. Deep-sea divers can know the ocean in ways only imagined by beachcombers.

This study uses a similar approach to the Scriptures. Each session begins with "On the Surface," a basic retelling of the Bible story. You will read what the Bible says and hear what that story might have sounded like to the first hearers of this Word. For some people, this might be enough.

But the next section, "Exploring the Depths," invites you to venture out a bit more and examine in depth what the Bible story might mean. What issues does this story bring up for us? What does the passage say to us about God or about ourselves?

The final section, "Diving In," basically examines how this passage of Scripture might change our lives if we were to really take it seriously. What help could we find for living a faith-filled life from this passage?

Each of the Bible studies we will explore has been chosen because it shows us yet another way of "diving in" to the coming realm of God. We will learn of Gideon and how he obeyed, even when he was unsure of his own abilities.

We will learn of David's kindness to Mephibosheth and how Jesus taught his disciples the importance of being forgiving. We will hear of the boldness of a woman who dared to reach out and get what she needed from Jesus. And finally, we will see how Jesus gave to Thomas what he needed to become a believer.

While these passages are placed in the sequence that they appear in the Bible, there is no need for you to study them in this order. Each session can stand on its own to be studied as the Holy Spirit inspires you.

We live in a world heavily influenced by a culture that tells us to put ourselves first before other people and to never even consider what God would have us do. In our consumer-driven world, we want to strive always to get ahead, to obtain a better lifestyle, to have the latest or the biggest or the flashiest model.

But when we read the Bible and then move into the depths of the Bible to hear how God would have us live, we can see how shallow our culture would have us be. To move from a lifestyle characterized by getting more and more "things" toward a lifestyle that would have us be more and more relational is truly revolutionary. Imagine if everyone put more value in the relationships we have with God and with one another than we do with amassing "wealth" and "security." We could literally change the world.

As I wrote this study, I was constantly mindful of you, the leader/learner. I prayed for you that you would come to know God more fully and would see others around you as precious children of God. May God bless your ministry as you dive into the depths of God's Word and God's Love.

Faithfully,
Linda Ray Miller

Ways to Use This Resource

Call of the Deep: Diving Into God's Way of Life is designed to be flexible. You can use it in many different settings:

- It can be used in an intergenerational learning setting, such as vacation Bible school. Each of the five sessions can last for two hours or longer. You will find a number of intergenerational activities at the end of each session, where adults and children can learn together.
- It can be used as an adults-only study. Each session can be condensed to 45–60 minutes. This could be a perfect resource for an adult Sunday school class or adult weekday Bible study. You could also spread each session across multiple weeks to get the full benefit of all of the activities.
- It can be used as an adults-only retreat. For example, you could schedule Session One for Friday evening; Sessions Two, Three, and Four for Saturday; and Session Five for Sunday morning. Be sure to add time for meals, recreation, and sleeping!
- It can be used for individual study. While you would no doubt gain much insight from studying *Call of the Deep: Diving Into God's Way of Life* with other participants, you can also use the suggested leader/learner helps in the gray boxes for your personal enrichment.

If you are planning to lead a group study, here are some helpful suggestions:

1. Read each session in advance. Some suggested activities require materials for the participants. For example, Session Four calls for you to bring pictures cut from magazines for closing worship. Session Five calls for you to prepare cotton balls soaked in smelly liquids.

2. Encourage the participants to read the session in advance. If everyone is prepared, the group discussion will be greatly enriched. Yet realize that, no matter what you say, some participants will not have read the assignment. Ask volunteers to summarize sections of the readings. Be prepared to summarize the reading yourself, just in case no one is prepared!

3. This is a Bible study. Each session refers to different passages of Scripture. Encourage the participants to bring a Bible with them, but also have several Bibles available. Some participants may forget to bring one from home, and others may not own a Bible. This study utilizes the New Revised Standard Version. If possible, have copies of this translation on hand.

4. Ask for help. Just because you are the designated leader of this study does not mean that you have to lead it alone. There are many suggested leader/learner helps. You may be comfortable leading some and uncomfortable leading others. Ask other people to help lead opening worship, games, drama, art, or other activities. Everyone will benefit.

5. Above all, pray. Pray for each session. Pray for yourself as leader. Pray for others you have asked to lead with you. Pray for the group members.

Are you ready? Dive in!

Diving Into Obedience

Focus: God calls us to make a better world for all creation. Obedience to God's call brings about a deeper relationship with God and others.

Gathering

Use the opening worship to clear your mind from the clutter of the day's activities and prepare your heart to hear what God wants you to hear.

Create a visual focus for your worship by placing a candle and an open Bible on a table. If you have a bulletin board or a blank wall, display a piece of paper with the word "Obey" written on it. To identify more closely with the theme of this study, print the word "Obey" on blue paper and trim the edges to look like a wave of water. You will add to this focus wall display each session.

Light the candle and read Jeremiah 7:23. Divide the group into twos or threes and discuss Jeremiah 7:23 and the title of this study, *Call of the Deep: Diving Into God's Way of Life*. What images come to mind? What does it mean to the participants to dive deeper into God's Word? After a few minutes of discussion, invite the participants to share some of the highlights of their discussion.

Pray together: "Holy God, diving deep is a scary prospect. We do not know what we will find as we explore the depths of your love. Remind us always of your loving presence with us as we hear your call to obedience."

On the Surface

During the time of the judges, there was no real leader in Israel. After the Israelites had ended their wandering in the desert and had come to live in the "Promised Land," Joshua helped the tribes divide up the land among themselves. Each tribe, or family group, determined their own rules for getting along with each other. There were leaders, but they basically led only their own family. It was a pretty good system. Except, of course, when enemies attacked them and took their food.

Unfortunately, the Israelite tribes at the time were experiencing attacks from other groups, particularly from the Midianites, a nomadic tribe mentioned several times in the Bible (Numbers 25:17; 31:2; Judges 6). It was a group of Midianite traders who took Joseph from the pit where his brothers had thrown him and sold him to Ishmaelites on their way to Egypt (Genesis 37:28). Moses fled to the land of Midian and married Zipporah, the daughter of Jethro, a priest of Midian (Exodus 2:11-22). During the time of Gideon, Midianites raided Israelite farms. They made successful use of camels, which enabled them to raid the settled lands and then quickly escape back into the desert. They would come into the Israelite territories whenever they wanted and take whatever caught their eye. Judges 6 describes the pillaging and its horrific effect on the Israelites.

> They would encamp against them and destroy the produce of the land, as far as the neighborhood of Gaza, and leave no sustenance in Israel, and no sheep or ox or donkey. For they and their livestock would come up, and they would even bring their tents, as thick as locusts; neither they nor their camels could be counted; so they wasted the land as they came in. Thus Israel was greatly impoverished because of Midian; and the Israelites cried out to the Lord for help. (verses 4-6)

Make a list of the qualities you expect from a leader. What kind of qualities would inspire you to follow their leadership?

The world of the Israelites needed change. And in true Old Testament fashion, God called a leader to come to the aid of the people. Now, if I had been the one to call a leader, I would have called someone brave and powerful and charismatic. Someone, say, like David. Now there is a leader! David would run out to confront a giant against impossible odds. He would defend his sheep from lions and wolves. David's sheep—and his people—could rest in the fact that David was watching over them. [See 1 and 2 Samuel.]

However, at this point in time, God called Gideon. Who was this Gideon? Was he brave and powerful like David? Well, at the beginning of the story, Gideon was hiding from the Midianites by processing his grain out of sight, down inside the wine pit. This pit would have been a large space where the Israelites would have thrown all of the grapes from the vineyard in order to crush them. It would have probably been tiled or bricked. Otherwise, the juice from the grapes would get soaked into the ground. It would have been a nice place, but underground—out of the flow of wind. Definitely not a place one would choose for hard labor like beating out grain.

The Israelites who first heard this story surely had to chuckle when the angel called Gideon a "mighty warrior" (Judges 6:12). A mighty warrior, hiding in a hole?

Everyone silently read Judges 6:11-18. Invite three participants to read aloud the parts of narrator, God, and Gideon. Read the Scripture passage aloud. What do you think or feel about Gideon's responses to God? Why? Have you ever wanted to argue with God? What was it like?

The dominant emotion we get from Gideon is one of fear! When God asked Gideon to cut down the pagan idol, he did it in the dark of night, so that no one would know it was him (6:27-32). Okay, so Gideon wasn't the bravest kid on the block. So, perhaps he was powerful? Nope! Gideon went on to explain that he was the youngest member of a family that was part of the weakest clan of his tribe. And his tribe was, itself, one of the minor tribes (6:15). Hardly leader-making material.

Okay, but surely Gideon was decisive. Wrong again! He told God he needed a sign to know for sure he was on the right track. Gideon told God to put dew on the fleece and let the ground be dry (Judges 6:37). When God gave him this sign, Gideon said, "Well just to make sure, give me another sign—this time the opposite of the first one." That time the fleece was to be dry and the ground was to be wet (6:39). God gave him this sign as well.

Now, I'm thinking that this sign of the fleece is a pretty good one. I would believe that God was with me, wouldn't you?

Read Judges 6:36-40. How do you respond to Gideon's request for signs from God? What does the story say to you about Gideon? About God?

The fearful Gideon was obedient to God. He called the troops together at a spring called Harod. God told Gideon, "The troops with you are too many for me to give the Midianites into their hand. Israel would only take the credit away from me, saying, 'My own hand has delivered me.' Now therefore proclaim this in the hearing of the troops, 'Whoever is fearful and trembling, let him return home' " (Judges 7:2-3). Two-thirds of his army went home. Gideon, who knew for sure that God was with him, could not reassure two-thirds of his army that they would be successful. He did, however, stay with the remaining 10,000 troops.

If that weren't enough, once again God instructed Gideon to reduce his army even further by sending soldiers home based upon how they drank water from the spring. God said to Gideon, "All those who lap the water with their tongues, as a dog laps, you shall put to one side; all those who kneel down to drink, putting their hands to their mouths, you shall put to the other side" (Judges 7:5). The 300 who lapped water like a dog became the army that would defeat the Midianites. Thus Gideon, the fearful but obedient leader, was left with a handful of reckless, fearless warriors.

Read Judges 7:1-8. How does this story strike you? What thoughts or feelings do you have about it? What elements do you find challenging? Appealing? Amusing? What do Gideon's actions say to you about his leadership skills? About God?

So here's the situation: We have this group of bullies who come in and rob, murder, and pillage. And God calls a cowardly weakling to change the world. Logical? No. God-like? Yes! God seems to call the least likely folks to change the world. Remember

Moses? [See Exodus 3.] Even David was the youngest son of Jesse and not seriously considered for presentation before Samuel (1 Samuel 16:6-13). As God told Samuel, "The LORD does not see as mortals see; they look on the outward appearance, but the LORD looks on the heart" (16:7b).

Gideon, though fearful, obeyed God and defeated the Midianites in the most unlikely way. Gideon did not lead a mighty army to force the Midianites to behave. He and an army of only 300 men tricked the Midianites with torches, jars, and trumpets (Judges 7:9-23). What a story!

> Read Judges 7:9-23. In what ways, if any, does this strategy for defeating the Midianites change your opinion about Gideon's leadership skills? What does it say to you about Gideon? About God? About obedience?

Exploring the Depths

Okay, great story and all, but what does it mean to us? What does it teach us about God and about ourselves? What can it tell us about obedience to God as a practice of our Christian lives? How might our obedience to God contribute to a better world?

First of all, we need to acknowledge that our world needs some changes. Our world contains corrupt politicians, folks who care more for making money than helping people, and people who would use terror to control us. People who are weaker and less powerful than us are suffering. Children's needs are being neglected. Scam artists and credit card companies are exploiting people. Families are losing their homes because they cannot afford their mortgage payments. Families are doing their best to hold together in the face of mental illness, addictions, and job losses. Illness or depression make it difficult for some people to get out of bed in the morning and put one foot in front of the other.

> Make a list of the changes that need to be made in your world. What is going on in your community? In your state? In your church family? In the world?

So who would God call to fix this mess? We want God to call the brave and powerful leaders. We want our governments to handle all of the problems we encounter. We want our religious leaders to go out and condemn those who would take advantage of us and make them stop. We want the media to uncover the corruption and force everyone to play fair. That's who we think God should call!

But who does God call to change the world? Not just the powerful, charismatic leaders. God calls *us*! God tells us that we cannot simply hide in the wine press and hope that somehow all of the bad things going on will somehow pass us by. God calls us to come out, to blow trumpets, to break some jars, and to shine some lights. It is no good telling God how unqualified we are. That strategy did not work for Gideon or any of the other unlikely leaders God called. God knows exactly who we are—all our fears, all our uncertainties, all our weaknesses. And God chooses us to change our world. Our obedience to God's call makes change possible.

> What qualities do you have that can help to change the world? Are you good at hospitality or problem solving? Are you patient with children? Are you good at writing and sending emails? Do you like to talk on the phone? Are you good at handling money? Make a list of the talents that God has given you. How might you use these qualities to make a difference in your church? In your community? In the world?

Diving In

Another thing to notice about Gideon's story is that he did not simply hear God's call and go out and act. Gideon was unsure of his own abilities to lead, and he was also unsure that where he was going was really where God wanted him to go. So, he asked God again and again for clarification (Judges 6:17, 36-40). And along the way, Gideon learned to pay attention to detail. He noticed where the dew was (6:36-40). He noticed how his followers drank water (7:4-7). He listened to the Midianites' conversation (7:9-14). Gideon went back to God time after time to check to make sure he was still on the right path.

The rewarding thing about going back to God time after time to check in is that we can't help but form a relationship. The more successful and productive relationships involve lots of communication between the parties. It never hurts to say, "God are you sure this is what you want me to do?" especially when, like Gideon, we wait to hear the answer and then obey God.

One thing that we need to remember about the story of Gideon is that he did not drive off the Midianites with his great power. He was not a brave and powerful military leader who used force to win the battle. Rather, he used what he had: jars, torches, and trumpets. And Gideon definitely did not get rid of bullies for all time to come. Every generation has had its own bullies and has needed leaders to help those who are weaker. God is calling us to do exactly what we can do with our own sets of skills and abilities. All we have to do is listen and obey. Consider the questions below.

- Is there someone in your world whose income level does not allow them to ever climb on top of their debt?

- Is there someone in your world who feels lonely and cut off from society?

- Are there children in your world who do not have a safe home environment?

- What other needs do you identify in your world?

We respond to such questions in many ways. Perhaps we are called to run for public office and change policies. Perhaps we are called to rock babies in a neonatal intensive care nursery or in a church nursery. Perhaps we are called to help a family on a limited income learn to plant a garden to supplement their food budget, to help a person on the brink of homelessness find affordable housing, or to spend an afternoon calling people on the telephone to let them know someone cares about them. The possibilities are endless because the needs are many. And when we obey God's call and offer ourselves to God's good in our world, we dive deeper into our own spiritual life.

Closing Worship

Gather together around your worship area. Give each participant an index card and an envelope. Make sure everyone has a writing utensil.

Sing "Lord, I Want to Be a Christian," "O Love That Wilt Not Let Me Go," "Take My Life, and Let It Be Consecrated," "Where He Leads Me," or another hymn of commitment.

Spend some time in silence reflecting on God's call for your life. Imagine that you are down inside of a wine press—or large hole in the ground. Imagine God as an angel on the edge of the hole, calling you to climb out and face your fears about changing your world. What will you say to God?

When you are ready, write a situation or a person's name on your card. This should be something or someone that you feel strongly that God is calling you to help change. Seal the card within the envelope and write your initials on the outside of the envelope. If you are willing to obey God's calling to help in this situation, lay your envelope on the worship center.

Pray: "O God, we are hesitant to obey. We really want you to call someone else—someone with more skill, or courage, or power. But we recognize your call to what we can in our world. Give us the strength and courage we need to obey your call. Amen."

INTERGENERATIONAL ACTIVITIES

Identify Problems and Solutions

Children can be great problem solvers when they are heard. And adults can help to guide them to make decisions that are actually practical and workable.

Make a list of problems in your world, like homelessness, lonely people at a retirement center, or feral cats in the neighborhood. Choose one and brainstorm solutions to the problem. Remember that in brainstorming, all ideas are valid. After all, who would have thought that broken pots and trumpets would have driven off an army?

Check in with God (pray) to see what solution would be practical and workable. Form a plan to make a change in your world. Remember to keep the planning and discussion open to all ages.

Begin a Work Project

Plan a project that will last the entire time of this study. For example, make "Paper Sack Lunches" to feed hungry people in your community. There are often folks standing on street corners with signs that say, "I'm hungry, please help." Some people are hesitant to give such people money but are very comfortable giving them a sack lunch. During the first session, make a list of items you will need and get volunteers to bring them. For example, canned tuna (in easy-open cans), packages of crackers, packaged fruit, cookies, and juice boxes. Make signs to place around your church enlisting people to bring the needed items during the time of your study. Plan what you would like to include in your lunches.

Play a Game

Gideon was obedient to what God wanted him to do. Practice obedience by playing "Simon Says." The person whose birthday is coming up next will begin. This person says, "Simon says, pat your head" (or another simple command that everyone in the group can perform). The group continues to follow the command until the leader says, "Simon says, clap your hands" (or another command). If the person simply issues a command without saying, "Simon says," the group is to ignore the command and keep on doing whatever the last command was. Keep playing until someone gets caught not doing what Simon says.

Paper Bag Dramas

Divide participants into groups of five or six people, making sure that each team has a representation of all ages involved in your study (for example, two children, one youth, one young adult, two senior adults). Give each team a paper grocery bag with five miscellaneous items in it (for example, a scarf, a cell phone, a plastic bowl, a plastic flower, and a devotional magazine). The items do not really matter, but should be as random as possible. Ask each group to act out the story of Gideon. The rules are: Every person on the team must participate and the team must use every prop in the bag for something. The teams will have ten minutes to prepare their skit. When they are finished, have each team act out their dramas for the entire group.

Write a Hymn

Choose a hymn with which everyone is familiar, such as "Amazing Grace." Count the number of syllables in each verse of the hymn. For example, "Amazing Grace" has eight syllables in the first verse, six syllables in the second verse, eight syllables in the third verse, and six syllables in the last verse. Now write a hymn about Gideon modeled after "Amazing Grace" that has eight syllables in the first verse, six in the second, etc. For example, "An angel came to Gideon" has eight syllables and will fit either the first verse or the third of "Amazing Grace." You may have to play with the word order for your hymn to sound good. "Gideon was beating the grain" also has eight syllables, but does not fit the tune as well. Sing your hymn together.

Make a Banner

Tape a large sheet of bulletin board paper to the wall. Have someone draw a figure of a man beating out grain on the sheet, and write "Be Obedient" in balloon letters across the top of the sheet. Take tissue paper and cut it into one-inch squares. Crumple each square, dip it into a dish of glue, and then paste it onto the banner. You will be "coloring" the picture with tissue paper. For example, one square of crumpled yellow or tan tissue paper should be glued onto each head of grain. Gideon's clothing should be all one color. Try to fill the entire banner with crumpled paper—or at least the figure of Gideon and the balloon letters. You will add a new picture at the end of each session.

Diving Into Kindness

Focus: Showing kindness to those who threaten us or who are different from us is difficult, but such kindness brings about a deeper relationship with God and others.

Gathering

Play soft music as the participants gather. Create a worship center by placing a candle and an open Bible on a table. Print the words "Be Kind" on blue paper and trim the edges to look like a wave of water. Add to your wall display or your bulletin board. You are adding to this focus wall display each session.

Light the candle and read Colossians 3:12. Divide the group into twos or threes and discuss the verse. What images come to mind? What does it mean to clothe oneself in kindness? After a few minutes of discussion, invite the participants to share some of the highlights of their discussion.

Pray together: "Holy God, we receive your blessings every day. But we do not always recognize them for what they are. Keep us ever mindful of our many blessings as we follow your command to be kind."

On the Surface

OK, let's be honest. Who has ever heard of Mephibosheth? Who can pronounce it correctly? [Muh-FIB-oh-shehth] And what can we learn from the story of David and Mephibosheth that will encourage our own spiritual growth?

Those who have done a detailed study of the life of King

Open your Bibles to 2 Samuel 9:1-13. Assign parts to participants and read the passage aloud. Have one person be David, one Ziba, one Mephibosheth, and one person be the narrator. Read the story aloud. What especially strikes you about the story? What makes you want to know more?

David know about Mephibosheth. To understand his story, you have to put your mindset back in the days of the ancient kings. We all know about the rights of succession for royalty. When a king or queen dies or steps down, the oldest son becomes king. If the oldest son is unable, or unwilling, the next oldest son becomes the king. In the absence of sons, the daughters are tapped to be queen. If no sons or daughters are available, the search is on amongst the blood relatives of the current monarch. In fact, if you can claim any blood lineage to the royal family, you, too, could be in line for the throne.

Of course, royal families change from time to time. If the current royal family is ousted, a new royal family can be named. But there is always the chance that folks loyal to the former royal family will keep things stirred up so that there is a chance that one of the "rightful" heirs to the kingdom will inherit. So in the interests of stable government, the sensible thing to do is to kill off anyone who has the remotest chance of inheriting the throne, even little babies. At least, that was the belief at the time of David.

When David was proclaimed king, instead of Saul, anyone connected to Saul was in danger. And, in fact, many of them were killed. But not all of them. David had a special connection to Saul's family. David's best friend was Jonathan, Saul's son (and supposed heir). Their friendship and love for each other was legendary. Even

Read 1 Samuel 19:1-7 and 20:1-42. Why do you think Jonathon went out of his way to be kind to David?

though Jonathan knew that David threatened his own inheritance, he went out of his way to protect David from the wrath of his father (1 Samuel 19:1-7; 20:1-42).

The relationship of these two men had little to do with envy or jealousy but was based on mutual trust and respect. Jonathan knew very well that his father feared the popularity of David and wanted him dead. And if Jonathan had an ambitious bone in his body, he would have helped Saul kill David long before. Remember, Jonathan was the supposed heir to the throne. To allow David to live meant that Jonathan's own future was in jeopardy.

> Have a participant read 1 Samuel 20:13-15 aloud. What connections do you see between this Scripture and the story of David and Mephibosheth?

When Saul and Jonathan were killed by the Philistines, and David was proclaimed king, David did not have the family of Saul killed automatically. In fact, when David learned of Saul's death, he composed a song and ordered all the people to learn it (2 Samuel 1:17-27). It is true that after several years David allowed the Gibeonites to kill seven sons of Saul (21:1-14), but David did not go out of his way to seek the family members of Saul and have them slaughtered. Perhaps David was secure enough in his own kingship that he felt he didn't need to do that. Perhaps he had enough of bloodshed and he just didn't want to go to the trouble. In any case, survivors of Saul's family were still around years later.

During the confusing time after the death of Saul and the ascension of David to the throne, we hear an account of Jonathan's five-year-old son, Mephibosheth, who is injured as his nurse carries him out of harm's way (2 Samuel 4:4). He is just a bit player in this drama surrounding King David and the struggle for the proper successor to his throne. He appears only a few times, but he has a powerful message for us.

After many years, David began wondering about the family of Jonathan. The last we heard, Mephibosheth was only five years old. David asked, "Is there still anyone left of the house of Saul to whom I may show kindness for Jonathan's sake?" (2 Samuel 9:1). The Hebrew word for *kindness* in this Scripture passage means more than being nice to someone. The word, *hesed*, suggests covenant loyalty. In 2 Samuel 9:3, David asks Ziba, a servant in the house of Saul, the same question with a slight difference: "Is there anyone remaining of the house of Saul to whom I may show the kindness of God?" David's loyalty to the covenant with Jonathan is likened to the loyalty of God. It also echoes the language of the covenant he had made with Jonathan. "If I am still alive, show me the faithful love of the LORD; but if I die, never cut off your faithful love from my house, even if the LORD were to cut off every one of the enemies of David

> What insights do you gain about the word *kindness* as it is used in 2 Samuel 9? What insights does it offer to you about the possibilities of human relationships? What insights does it offer to you about God?

from the face of the earth" (1 Samuel 20:14-15). The words *faithful love* are translations of the same word in the original Hebrew, *hesed*. In both cases, the word carries the meanings of mercy, lovingkindness, and faithfulness. And in both cases, the word is associated with God.[1]

Ziba told David that Mephibosheth was alive. He was now an adult and had a son of his own (2 Samuel 9:12). David brought Mephibosheth to the palace and greeted him like a long-lost relative. Why would he do this? After all, Mephibosheth was a direct descendant of Saul through Jonathan, Saul's successor. While he was lame and therefore probably posed no threat to the throne, he was able bodied enough to have fathered a son who would be yet another threat to David's authority. But David not only spared Mephibosheth's life, he provided generously for him and his family.

> What do you think about the motives for David's actions toward Mephibosheth?

This action was incomprehensible to the politically savvy of the time. The prudent thing—if David did not want to kill Mephibosheth—was at least to downplay his connection to the royal lineage. But David gave Mephibosheth all that belonged to Saul, underscoring that lineage. Further, he gave Ziba responsibility for managing the household.

Most people would have looked at Mephibosheth and seen only threat. If he had chosen, Mephibosheth could have claimed that he was the rightful king and members of Saul's tribe could have risen up in rebellion and tried to put himself or his son on the throne. But David looked beyond the threat when he looked at Mephibosheth. Instead of a threat, he saw Jonathan's son. Instead of a royal usurper, David saw a small child injured in the panic that came after the death of his father and grandfather. Instead of someone who was trying to bring about David's downfall, David saw a man who had lost everything that had belonged to his family and who needed protection and safety.

To Mephibosheth, this kindness was totally unexpected. Mephibosheth surely knew his place—and his danger. He must have been told that his lame feet were a result of his nurse trying to get him out of harm's way after the ascension of David to the throne. But Mephibosheth bowed down before David and referred to himself as a dead dog (2 Samuel 9:8). He knew that he had no rights, no security, and no expectation of kindness.

But kindness was just what he got. David was not only kind to Mephibosheth, he was overly kind. He spared his life; he gave to Mephibosheth everything that had belonged to Saul; and he also treated Mephibosheth like one of his own sons, allowing him to live in Jerusalem and eat at the king's table. This goes beyond what David was called on to do. After all, what he promised was to "never cut off [his] faithful love to [Jonathan's] house" (1 Samuel 20:15). He hadn't agreed to anything about setting up Mephibosheth like one of his own family.

> Have you ever had an opportunity to honor a friend or family member by showing kindness to their children? If so, when? What was the occasion? What did you learn? How did you feel? What was God's role?

David's servants and family must have thought he was crazy. According to the political standards of the day, one would expect a king to kill those who threatened him. Second Samuel 9 shows David as one who honored his covenant with Jonathan and who demonstrated through these actions the loyal, lovingkindness of God. He did what he thought was the right thing, without apology, out of love for God and out of his desire to keep his promise to his great friend, Jonathan.

Exploring the Depths

So this story is not about Mephibosheth at all. He just happens to be the one with the unusual name. This story is about David and his actions. How can we use this incident in David's life to find ourselves in a closer relationship with God and others? Generally speaking, most of us are not royalty and we do not have to worry about getting rid of our enemies so that our future is secure. It would be easy to say that this Bible story does not apply directly to our lives. If we, however, look beyond the surface of the story and explore its depths, we can see connections.

Name one word or one phrase from this story that connects with your life and inspires you to closer relationship with God and with others. Invite others in your group to do the same. Make a list by writing these words and/or phrases on newsprint or a whiteboard for all to see.

Our culture today teaches us that life is all about winning. We learn it in Little League when we are preschoolers. Teachers will tell you that one of the best ways to motivate kids to action is to set up a competition. One of the worst things you can call a child or a youth is a loser.

While competition can inspire and motivate people, it has a darker side. Anyone who knows me well knows that I understand very little about sports. But in the interest of school spirit, and a love of marching bands, I have often gone to Friday night high school football games. I clearly remember one game in particular. The quarterback threw the ball too far, and it hit the ground for an instant before being scooped up by a linebacker. However, the referee did not see the ball hit the ground. I knew enough to know that once the ball hit the ground, it was supposed to be out of play. But everyone around me seemed to think that the linebacker got a lucky break. (The play *did* help our team.) It sure looked like cheating to me. When I commented on this, my companions rolled their eyes and patiently explained that I just did not understand football: If the referee did not see it—it did not happen. I remarked that if my son ever caught that "lucky break" I would expect him to confess. (More rolled eyes.) According to them, I simply did not understand the way the game worked.

But I think I did understand. This game was teaching the prevailing view of our culture, which values winning. I often wonder how many people believe the adage, "It matters not if you win or lose, but how you play the game." Look at the popular reality shows on television: *Survivor* and its sequels show us how to use trickery and cunning to get other folks kicked off of "the island." *The Apprentice* shows us that nice guys (and girls) will never succeed in business. It seems that the meaner and nastier the participants are, the more we enjoy watching them.

In this climate, kindness is not only unrewarded, it is actively discouraged. We see news coverage of parents fighting over the last hot toy for Christmas giving—completely missing the point of Christmas in the first place. We have to be number one at all costs. A coach whose team is consistently "number two" will find him or herself looking for another job. In the book *Tuesdays With Morrie*, Mitch Albom describes his relationship with an older professor, who taught him much more than sociology. One of my favorite passages is when Morrie overhears students cheering, "We're number one!" He stops them and asks, "What's wrong with being number two?"[2]

Being nice or kind does not seem to be part of our culture. It would seem that being kind is for kindergartners and

> Do you agree or disagree with the message that kindness is for losers? What examples from your own life can you use to illustrate your point?

must be unlearned by the time we are in competition for the best schools, the best jobs, or the largest houses. Being kind is more apt to lose us votes, sales, or other rewards than it is to help us get ahead in life.

But doesn't Jesus teach us that the opposite is true? "Whoever wants to be first must be last of all and servant of all" (Mark 9:35b). What kind of logic is that? Is Jesus trying to say to us that if we serve others, we will be successful? Well, that must be by God's standards and not the world's.

Jesus tells us again and again that being number one (by the world's standards) is not the measure of success by God's standards. In Matthew 5:39-40, Jesus says, "Do not resist an evildoer. But if anyone strikes you on the right cheek, turn the other also; and if anyone wants to sue you and take your coat, give your cloak as well." Can't you just hear Donald Trump saying, "You're fired!"? God clearly has a different definition of success. Jesus' vision is grander than getting ahead in this life. Read again the Beatitudes (5:3-11). Can you imagine quoting anything from this passage in business school? "Blessed are the meek; blessed are the merciful." These actions are rarely rewarded by our culture. So, to follow the example of King David's treatment of Mephibosheth and the example of Jesus is completely counter-cultural. Yet, we are called to do so. Even within our culture we can hear the call to kindness. One of Glen Campbell's classic songs tells us to "try a little kindness" and "shine [our] light for everyone to see."[3]

Diving In

It is easy to be kind to some people. We already have a relationship with people such as our spouse, our children, our best friend, our pastor, to name a few. We can probably anticipate them being kind to us in return. It is also easy to be kind to folks who look like us, think like us, and agree with our opinions. We understand these people. They understand us. Kindness and thoughtfulness come naturally with people who are like us.

> Where do you hear and see the call to kindness in our culture?

On the other hand, what about someone who is not like us? Someone who disagrees with us? And what about someone who could threaten us? What about the person who joins our team and could potentially be after our job? What about a person who is out to swindle us? Someone who disagrees with our style of parenting and does not hesitate to point it out? What about the company gossip? The emotionally needy person at church? Do we really have to be kind to them, too?

Being kind to those who are kind to us is easy. But to be kind to someone who does not deserve it, or someone we do not know or like, is just plain hard. Of course, there are seasons when it is easier to be kind—like at Christmas. Kindness is generally seen as positive during the holiday season at the end of the year. During the month of December, we can provide food and gifts for needy families, tip a little more generously, hold the door

> Toward which people in your world is it difficult, if not impossible, to show kindness? Telemarketers? Criminals? Domineering people? People who are always right? Always smarter than you are? Homeless persons? Others?

for someone on crutches. But on January 1, it's back to business as usual. Kindness is what we want from others, but do we have to give it to others?

Whoops! That reminds us of another one of Jesus' sayings. Remember the one about doing to others as you would have them do to you? That one is found in Matthew 7:12. Jesus is determined to make us focus on others, isn't he?

Kindness helps us to see other people as fully human. As long as we are focused on ourselves and our own goals and dreams, other people can be seen as obstacles or steppingstones to our personal achievement. But if we stop to notice the person, note what needs they may have, and strive to meet those needs with kindness, we are able to see them as God does—as beloved children of God.

And when we truly see other people as beloved children of God, we can recognize even more the love that God has toward us. When we can turn our focus away from ourselves and our own needs, we can rejoice in our own blessings and pass them on to others. To focus on being kind to everyone—and I mean everyone—will help us move from the self-serving model taught to us by the prevailing culture to becoming more like Christ in all that we do.

Think about it. Trying to "look out for number one," or always seeing others as obstacles in the way of getting what we want (and deserve!), does not make us happier. In fact, it may make us paranoid. But looking out for others, trying to find ways to be kind to them, and then noticing their response, makes life so much more pleasant. Trying kindness may mean letting the other driver get ahead of us on the freeway, smiling at the overworked cashier at the grocery store, or sitting beside the homeless person who enters our church sanctuary. Such small acts of kindness help lower our blood pressure and promote harmony in our world. If we really look at those who are different from us or who may threaten us in some way, chances are we will find another child of God who has bought into the prevailing culture and is truly not happy with it. Perhaps our acts of kindness can inspire others to also be kind. This could set off a chain reaction and make the world a better place for us all.

> Name some specific ways we can practice kindness. List these on newsprint or whiteboard for all to see. How do you think such acts of kindness will make a difference to those we meet daily? To ourselves? In our relationship with God?

David's treatment of Mephibosheth added yet another dimension to the practice of kindness. Remember the Hebrew word *hesed*? In the story, it is closely associated with the kindness, mercy, and loyalty of God. It is God's nature to show lovingkindness. David's kindness to Mephibosheth demonstrated the loyal kindness of God, and our kindness to others can do the same. Those who experience our kindness may experience a glimpse of the nature of God. Kindness brings us closer to one another and closer to God.

Closing Worship

Gather together around your worship area. If it is not still burning, light the candle as a sign of God's presence.

Sing "Lord, I Want to Be a Christian," "O Love That Wilt Not Let Me Go," "Take My Life, and Let It Be Consecrated," "Where He Leads Me," or another hymn of commitment.

Spend some time in silence reflecting on God's call to be kind. What would it mean to your life if you were to clothe yourself in kindness (Colossians 3:12)?

When you are ready, share your thoughts with one other person in your group. Make a commitment to be kind to one other person before you gather again. Ask for God's help, particularly if you are called upon to be kind to someone who you feel threatens you or to whom it is difficult to be kind.

Pray: "O God, we know you call us to be kind, but sometimes it is really hard. Our culture tells us to look out for ourselves and make sure no one gets the better of us. Help us as we strive to be kind to everyone we meet. Amen."

INTERGENERATIONAL ACTIVITIES

Continue a Work Project

Read the instructions for the work project in Session One. This week, continue to assemble the "sack lunches." Have participants decorate paper bags, write notes of support to include in the lunches, and then stuff them with one of each items you have collected. Plan a method of distribution. You may decide to take all of your sack lunches to a shelter. You may decide to place the sack lunches in a place where church members can take them to keep in their car.

Play a Game

Remember how David was kind to Mephibosheth by playing a relay game with a twist? Divide into three groups: two groups of taller people and one group of shorter people. Lay out an obstacle course with chairs and tables. For a challenge, have the course go over or under a table. The object of the game is to get all of the shorter people from one end of the course to the other without them using their legs. Two taller people will face each other and will grasp each other's right elbow with their left hand. They will grasp their own left elbow with their right hand. They will pick up the shorter person and carry them through the obstacle course. Only one team may be on the course at a time. Time your group to see how fast you can get all of the shorter people to the opposite end of the obstacle course. If desired, play again and try to improve your time. Playing against time, rather than against another team, promotes cooperation and teamwork.

Act It Out

Divide into four groups, making sure that there are people of all ages in each group. Assign each group one of the following characters: David's servant, David's son, Mephibosheth's former nurse, Mephibosheth's wife. Each group should prepare a short skit to show how their assigned character would have reacted upon hearing the news that David had asked Mephibosheth to move to Jerusalem and eat at the king's table. Each member of the group should have an assignment. Some could be furniture or have another non-speaking role.

Write a Hymn

Read the instructions for writing a hymn in Session One. Write a new verse about David and Mephibosheth. Make sure there is something in your stanza about being kind, which will help participants remember the purpose of this lesson.

Make a Banner

Tape a large sheet of bulletin board paper to the wall. Have someone draw a figure of a king standing, handing a plate to a man sitting on the ground. Write "Be Kind" in balloon letters across the top of the sheet. Read the instructions for "coloring" this picture in Session One. When finished, place this new picture next to the picture of Gideon. Leave room for other pictures of the stories to come. You will be creating a whole wall of pictures that will help participants remember the key points of the Bible stories and the purpose of each lesson.

[1] *The New Interpreter's Bible*, Vol. 2 (Abingdon Press, 1998); page 1273.
[2] Albom (Doubleday, 1997); page 159.
[3] From the song, "Try a Little Kindness," on *The Very Best of Glen Campbell* (Capitol Records, 1990).

Diving Into Forgiveness

Focus: Forgiveness is often hard, even when we know that we have been forgiven. Practicing forgiveness brings about a deeper relationship with God and others.

Gathering

Create a worship center by placing a candle and an open Bible on a small table. Print the words "Be Forgiving" on blue paper and trim the edges to look like a wave of water. Add to your wall display or your bulletin board. You are adding to this focus wall display each session.

Light the candle and read Ephesians 4:32. Divide the group into twos or threes and discuss the following questions: "What is the difference between being kind, being tenderhearted, and being forgiving? Is forgiveness harder than being kind? Why or why not?" After a few minutes, invite the participants to share some of the highlights of their discussion with the entire group.

Pray together: "Holy God, we know that we are supposed to be forgiving. We also know that you have forgiven us of so much. But God, it is hard to move from knowing to doing. Help us as we struggle to be forgiving people. Amen."

On the Surface

When I became a youth director, I began to realize that rules, by themselves, are worthless. Almost any rule I could come up with could be gotten around by clever youth. "Don't sit on the tables? OK, I will stand on the tables." "No food in the sanctuary? Then we should never have Communion again!" I finally got to the point where I told my youth group that there is only one rule: "Linda Ray has to have a good time! If I am chasing kids out of places they should not be, or stopping behavior that you know good and well is inappropriate, I am not having a good time." Note: "inappropriate" is a good word to use with youth. Much better than "wrong." Everyone knows what is appropriate in a given situation, but they can argue with you over whether or not it is "wrong." Youth need limits. We all need limits. But sometimes, rules just don't work.

When have you discovered that rules alone are ineffective for controlling behavior? How did you handle things? How did you establish limits? What worked best for you?

We see an example of the need for limits in the verses that come immediately before the Scripture for today's session about the unforgiving servant. Peter asked Jesus, "Lord, if another member of the church sins against me, how often should I forgive? As many as seven times?" (Matthew 18:21).

Read Matthew 18:21-22. What limits do you see in Peter's question? How does Jesus respond?

Peter questions Jesus, just as my youth group did. "So, Jesus, if someone does something bad to me, I am supposed to forgive them, right? But what if they do it again? Do I have to forgive them that time? And then, if they do it again and again? I mean, isn't there some sort of limit to all of this? How about seven times? I mean folks could seriously take advantage of you if they know you will just forgive them no matter what they do."

Jesus responds to Peter, "I do not say to you seven times, but seventy times seven" (18:22, RSV). In other words, there is an unlimited number of times that you should forgive someone who wrongs you!

The truth is, Peter was being generous with the number seven. Forgiving someone seven times is a dramatic reversal of the "sevenfold vengeance" pronouncement regarding Cain in Genesis 4:15. And Jesus went even further, reversing Lamech's "seventy-sevenfold" vengeance mentioned in Genesis 4:24. Both Peter and Jesus present a contrast between vengeance and forgiveness. Life according to God's way is not about vengeance. It's about forgiveness. And Jesus says, in essence, that it's not about counting either. Forgiveness is beyond limits and beyond rules. To illustrate his point about forgiveness, Jesus tells a story.

Imagine a kingdom. The king decides to conduct an audit of his accounts. He discovers that a servant owes him 10,000 talents. A talent was the amount paid for over 15 years of labor. Herod the Great received 900 talents a year in taxes from all his territories.[1] The amount that the servant owed the king was huge. There was no way this man could pay the king back. So, the king decided to repossess everything that the man owned, and since even that was not enough to cover the debt, he planned to sell the man and his entire family into slavery. This was definitely the king's right according to the law of the land at the time. After all, if you borrow money you should be able to pay it back.

> Invite two people to read Matthew 18:23-27. One person should read the words of Jesus. The other should read the words of the slave. How do you respond to the actions of the king toward the servant? Think about a huge debt, such as a mortgage or a credit card at its limit. What would it be like if the mortgage or credit card company wrote a letter saying the debt was no longer owed? What do these illustrations of forgiven debts say to you about God?

Punishment loomed for the servant; and he fell down before the king and pleaded with him, "Have patience with me, and I will pay you everything" (Matthew 18:26). The king had pity on him and decided to forgive him his debt. Did you get that? He didn't just have patience with the servant but totally wrote off this enormous debt! Rather than punishment, the servant received forgiveness.

Had the story stopped here, we would have a wonderful parable about God's generous grace. And the immensity of the forgiven debt certainly provides a concrete example to use as an illustration of God's grace. But in Matthew's Gospel, Jesus continued the story. He told about the reaction of the forgiven servant.

What would you expect this servant to do with his good fortune? I don't know about you, but when something especially nice happens to me, it makes me feel good all over. And when I feel good all over, I tend to be extra nice to everyone I come into contact with. This is a variation on, "When Mama's happy, everybody's happy." Kind of a "pass the love around" mentality. We would expect the servant, in gratitude, to go out and treat others with the same generosity of spirit demonstrated to him.

But what happened? He went out and came across another servant that owed him 100 denarii, which is about 100 days' wages.[2] While the amount was not a small one for the servant who owed it, when contrasted to the amount that the forgiven servant owed, it seems tiny. It is reasonable to assume that the amount could have been paid back. Like the king, the forgiven servant demanded that the person pay him what he owed. In an ironic parallel, the debtor fell down and pleaded with him in the same way that the forgiven servant had pleaded with the king. Even the words are the same: "Have patience with me, and I will pay you" (Matthew 18:29). Although it is reasonable that the debt could have been repaid, the forgiven servant did not give his fellow servant the mercy that he experienced; but instead had him thrown into prison. The first servant received mercy even though he owed thousands of times more money than the second servant. The second servant received punishment, even though his debt was, by comparison, just a trifle. Where's the fairness in that? So far so good. We understand that the forgiven servant is unjust and unforgiving, and we are offended by his actions. The first hearers must have thought the same thing. This is not fair! But Jesus continues the story.

So, the story goes on. Bystanders see what is going on and run to tell the lord of the injustice of the first servant. And the ending

> Have three people read the parts for Jesus, the forgiven servant, and the fellow servant in Matthew 18:28-30. What is your response to the actions of the first servant toward the one who owes him money? What insights do you gain about the story based upon the amounts owed?

is totally satisfying. The evil slave gets just what he deserves—eternal torment. Notice that he is not just thrown into jail, he is given over to tormenters. Jesus' story ends just the way we think it ought to. The bad guy got it in the end. But wait! Jesus told stories to teach us about God. So, if the "lord" in this story is supposed to be God, what does it mean for us? Does God take back forgiveness if we do not measure up? Does God's forgiveness come with strings attached? If Jesus' story is meant to be allegorical, or an example of how God acts, then we have to deal with the image of a vengeful God.[3] What do we do here? How should we hear these verses?

> Have two people read the parts for Jesus and the king in Matthew 18:31-35. What challenges you in this Scripture? How does it speak to you about fairness? About vengeance? About forgiveness?

Look again. The unforgiving servant was not punished for the debt he owed. He was punished for his refusal to *forgive* another. Did you get it? The unforgiving servant was forgiven for his enormous debt, but he was not forgiven for his refusal to forgive a pittance, for his unforgiving attitude. In other words, says Jesus, forgiveness is more important to God than money—even more money that you could ever see in your lifetime. Read Micah 6:6-8. God does not want "ten thousands of rivers of oil"—or tens of millions of dollars. God wants us to love kindness and to forgive one another. It's not about money. It's not about vengeance. It's about forgiveness.

Exploring the Depths

OK, this story is a little over the top, but isn't that the way Jesus is? He is trying to make a point here. It's not so much about *how much* is forgiven or even *how often* someone is forgiven. Jesus intentionally uses absurd numbers. And remember he is not reporting the facts in a legal case here. He is answering Peter's question.

Peter is asking a real question here. He wants to know what the limits are for forgiveness, when the person needing forgiveness is a member of your church. Apparently, he believes that there are different standards for church members. After all, if church members are like family, as opposed to enemies, the rules for forgiveness ought to be different. We need to be a little more forgiving when they are part of our "group." When someone is a friend, or a church member, we ought to forgive them. But how much? What if they really intended to do you harm? What if they aren't sorry? What if they have already done it once before and promised they would never do it again? What if they did the same thing seven times?

These are the kinds of questions we continue to ask today. How do we behave in relationship to others? What happens when someone that you consider a friend wrongs you? What are the limits of behavior. When do you get to stop forgiving them and kick them out of the group?

My great-uncle once came across the minutes of a small church in his community. These minutes spanned years in the early twentieth century. He told us that the interesting thing was how often some church members got kicked out of the church membership. Someone would become intoxicated, and the church would vote to kick him out. The next month, he would get "saved" again and be voted back into church membership. A couple of months later he would "backslide" and be kicked out again. Another person would beat up his wife and get kicked out and then be admitted back once he had repented of his sin. This happened to several members of this particular church. But, my uncle told us that no matter how many times a person got "kicked out," they were always voted back in as soon as they repented.

My question at the time was (and continues to be today), "Did it help the individual to get kicked out and then be forgiven?" What about the person they harmed, such as the battered wife? Would there have been better ways of handling these parishioners' behavior? Remember this was before the days of Alcoholics Anonymous or battered women's shelters.

Forgiveness has to do with people and relationships. Actions in and of themselves can be damaging, hurtful, and life-threatening;

and forgiveness does not mean allowing oneself to endure such actions. Using biblical teachings about forgiveness to tell someone to remain in an abusive relationship is a misuse of Scripture and a misunderstanding of

What standards of behavior exist in your church? Are there limits to the behavior for church members? Why or why not? Do you know of churches in your area that have stricter or more lenient behavior standards than your church does? How do these standards connect to the act of forgiveness? To God's forgiveness? To our forgiving others?

God. The point is that God wants us to forgive. Period. Not only when we are forgiven; not only when it's the first, or second, or third time. Not only when the person is really, really sorry. But *every* time someone wrongs you. This is where my grandfather would say that we have "stopped preachin' and gone to meddlin.' " Being obedient is a great concept: figure out what God wants and then do it. And being kind is all well and good. It gives us that warm fuzzy feeling. But being forgiving? I don't think so. You see, in order to be forgiving, first you have to be wronged. And it seems that God would be all about fairness. Let the other person be obedient and kind, and then we wouldn't have to be forgiving.

How was the little country church following Jesus' admonition to forgive? Where was it missing the mark? What kinds of behavior should be tolerated, and what should be admonished or stopped? Does forgiveness mean tolerating abusive behavior?

The limitless forgiveness taught by Jesus is difficult and challenging; however, such forgiveness leads to healing and wholeness. The good news is that God can do what we cannot do. And God empowers us to do what we need to do. In God's way of life, forgiveness leads to healing for the one who forgives. It may lead to healing for the one we forgive, or it may not. We cannot control that person's response, or that person may be deceased or no longer in our daily lives. It helps to think of forgiveness as a process empowered by God. When our intent is to forgive and when we pray for the capacity to forgive, we open our hearts and minds to

What thoughts or feelings do you have about the difficulty of forgiveness? What situations in your life or in the life of someone you know challenge Jesus' teaching about limitless forgiveness? How do you respond to the idea of forgiveness as a process empowered by God?

God's healing power and presence. Over time, we may notice that we are, in fact, being healed. Our feelings toward the one we need to forgive may become less intense. We do not have to do the work of forgiveness alone. God is with us.

Diving In

Jesus says, "Forgive." It doesn't matter how much. It doesn't matter how often. We are called to be forgiving people. Why? Because if we are honest, we will recognize how very much we have been forgiven, both by God and by the people who love us. And to pass that forgiveness along will help us to grow closer to the mind and heart of God.

But God knows that our human nature finds it hard to forgive. Our first impulse in every case is to retaliate. We want to recite the Golden Rule as: "Do unto others exactly as they do unto you." And God understands that.

As a group, make a list of people we are called to forgive. List the people by category, not by name. For example, "Drunk Drivers," "Rude Sales Clerks," etc. Put each category on a sticky note and then rate them according to how easily they can be forgiven. This exercise is meant as a discussion starter. Each instance will bring its own unique details and each participant will have his or her own unique viewpoint, and so your list will constantly change.

We can start with small things. We can forgive those little irritants that happen every day—the person who cuts us off in traffic, the person who doesn't notice that we held the door open for them, the person who ticks us off for no reason at all. Surely we can get past this one. As we practice forgiving persons who have irritated us, we can learn the skills necessary to forgive those who have really wronged us.

I have found that four words serve me well when I need to forgive. These words are: relax, relate, rehearse, and release. Easy to remember but still hard to do.

RELAX. I was taught as a child to count to ten every time I felt angry. This is still good advice, as long as we are actually counting slowly in order to calm ourselves down, rather than using it as a countdown to really let them have it. Take a deep breath. Try to slow the beating of your heart. Take a step back from the situation so that you can really see what is going on. Is it really all that important to be at the front of the line? Or be able to drive at the speed you want to go? Or to be thanked for every good deed that you do? Perhaps your feeling of being wronged comes from the fact that you really are having a bad day. Practicing relaxation when you are starting to get angry can truly help.

RELATE. We need to try and put ourselves in the other person's shoes. Have we ever inadvertently cut someone off in traffic? If we drive, of course we have. Sometimes we aren't paying attention. Perhaps we have a true emergency and really do need to get somewhere fast. (I'm not talking about being the first in the cafeteria line—I mean real emergency, like involving blood or imminent death!) Perhaps the person who cut us off really does have an emergency. We never know.

REHEARSE. Several years ago, I read a quotation from C. S. Lewis that profoundly changed my life on several levels. "Do not waste time bothering whether you 'love' your neighbour [sic]; act as if you did. As soon as we do this we find one of the great secrets. When you are behaving as if you loved someone, you will presently come to love him."[4] The same is true for forgiveness. If we want to forgive someone, we can try acting as if we had already forgiven him or her. In other words, *rehearse* forgiveness. What would it look like if we truly forgave someone? What would it feel like? How might we behave differently toward that person? And if we keep on rehearsing, we will presently discover that we have, in fact, forgiven them.

RELEASE. Once we have forgiven, we must release our anger, our grudges, our impulses to retaliate. Releasing means not watching the other person to see when they are going to injure us again. Releasing means being able to see the other person without first seeing the wrong they have done to us. Releasing means being free of the anger that boils up in us when we have been wronged.

Relax, relate, rehearse, and release. Sounds simple, but as we all know, it is incredibly difficult. In fact, it is almost impossible without God's help. But because of Jesus' parable of the unforgiving servant, we know that God wants us to do it. And, logically, if God wants us to do something, we will discover that we have the tools and the abilities to do it.

Closing Worship

Gather together around your worship area. Give each participant an index card and an envelope. Make sure everyone has a pen or pencil.

Sing "Lord, I Want to Be a Christian," "O Love That Wilt Not Let Me Go," "Take My Life, and Let It Be Consecrated," "Where He Leads Me," or another hymn of commitment.

Spend some time in silence reflecting on today's lesson. Write on your note card things you have been forgiven of, both small and large. Reflect on your list, and give thanks for every instance of forgiveness. Next write down persons whom you need to forgive for wrongs they have done to you. Pray and ask God to give you the strength to forgive them.

Pray: "O God, forgiveness is hard. Nothing in our culture prepares us to forgive. But the experience of receiving forgiveness from you compels us to forgive others. Help us as we pray the prayer you taught us to pray, saying 'Our Father in heaven, hallowed be your name. . . .' Amen."

INTERGENERATIONAL ACTIVITIES

Continue a Work Project

Read the instructions for the work project in Session One. This week, continue to assemble the "sack lunches." Have participants decorate paper bags, write notes of support to include in the lunches, and then stuff them with the items you have collected. Begin your distribution, if you have not already done so. Plan to gather reports of how the lunches were distributed and what was the reaction of the one who received the lunch (if known). You may decide to take all of your sack lunches to a shelter. You may decide to place the sack lunches in a place where church members can take them to keep in their car.

Play a Game

Forgiveness Pantomime

Write the following phrases on individual sheets of paper. Use the phrases to play a game of pantomime. Tell the participants that you will be pantomiming Bible verses that have to do with forgiveness. In order to keep this game from being a competition, simply pass out the verses to individuals to act out and then let the whole group try to guess the Bible verse.

- Blessed are the merciful, for they will receive mercy. (Matthew 5:7)
- If anyone strikes you on the right cheek, turn the other also. (Matthew 5:39b)
- Forgive us our debts, as we also have forgiven our debtors. (Matthew 6:12)
- Be merciful, just as your Father is merciful. (Luke 6:36)
- Forgive, and you will be forgiven. (Luke 6:37b)
- Father, forgive them; for they do not know what they are doing. (Luke 23:34)

Write a Hymn

Read the instructions for writing a hymn in Session One. Write a new verse about the unforgiving servant. Make sure there is something in your stanza about being forgiving to help participants remember the purpose of this lesson.

Make a Banner

Tape a large sheet of bulletin board paper to the wall. Have someone draw a figure of two people hugging, and write "Be Forgiving" in balloon letters across the top of the sheet. Read the instructions for "coloring" the picture in Session One. Try to fill the entire sheet with crumpled tissue paper. Place this new picture alongside the others. Leave room for other pictures of the stories to come. You will be creating a whole wall of pictures that will help participants remember the key points of the Bible stories and the purpose of each lesson.

---

[1] See *The New Interpreter's Bible,* Vol. 8 (Abingdon Press, 1995); page 382.

[2] See note 1 above.

[3] See discussion of Matthew's use of allegory in the parable in *The New Interpreter's Bible*, Vol. 8; page 382–83. See also *The New Interpreter's Study Bible* (Abingdon Press, 2003); pages 1779–80.

[4] *Mere Christianity*, by C. S. Lewis (Macmillan, 1952); page 101.

Diving Into Boldness

Focus: Even when we know what we want, we sometimes lack the courage to go after it. Boldness brings about a deeper relationship with God and others.

Gathering

Create a worship center by placing a candle and an open Bible on a small table. Print the words "Be Bold" on blue paper and trim the edges to look like a wave of water. Add to your wall display or your bulletin board. You are adding to this focus wall display each session.

Light the candle and read 1 John 5:14. Divide the group into twos or threes and discuss the verse. Could we really ask for anything and expect to receive it? After a few minutes, invite the participants to share some of the highlights of their discussion.

Pray together: "Holy God, boldness does not always seem to be a Christian virtue. We are more likely to be humble and subservient. And yet, we know that we are also called to be bold in order to bring about change in our world."

On the Surface

Luke 8 presents three healing stories in which Jesus reached across religious and cultural boundaries in order to respond to human need. Luke 8:26-39 tells us that Jesus cast out demons from a man who was living

Assign one person to be the woman, one person to be Peter, one person to be Jesus, and one person to be the narrator. Have the participants read aloud Luke 8:40-48. What words or phrases stand out for you in this passage? What do you think was going through the mind of Jairus? Of Jesus? Of the woman? Of Peter? Of those who were in the crowd that pressed in on Jesus? If you have time, have the readers assume the roles of the parts they read aloud and have them respond, in character, to the preceding questions.

49

in the tombs in the country of the Gerasenes. Luke 8:40-56 tells the story of two healings. A leader in the synagogue named Jairus begged Jesus to come to his house and to heal his dying twelve-year-old daughter. Jesus agreed; and as he moved through the crowds, a woman in the crowd reached out and touched the fringe of his clothing.

Something happened when the woman touched Jesus' clothing. Jesus felt power go out of him and he stopped. "Who touched me?" he asked. The disciples must have thought that this was a peculiar question because Jesus was surrounded by people. Many people might have touched him in such a crowd. And shouldn't Jesus have known who touched him? If he did know, why did he make a big deal out of it? Couldn't he have acknowledged the healing silently? Couldn't he have smiled knowingly at the woman, as if they shared a great secret? In other healing stories, he told people to keep the healing a secret (Luke 8:56). The woman, who probably would have preferred to remain unnoticed, knew that Jesus was referring to her. She came forward with fear and trembling, fell down in front of Jesus, and confessed that she had touched his clothing and had been healed.

Why do you think Jesus asked who touched him? Why do you think the woman was trembling?

So who was this woman? Like many of the women in the Bible, she is not named. But we know that she was sick. She didn't just have a fever, or a headache—she had an issue of blood that she had lived with for 12 years! We don't know the exact nature of her malady; but because it was a flow of blood, she would have been considered to be ritually unclean. And of course, she could have been menstruating. According to Scripture, anyone who even accidentally touched a menstruating woman would be ritually unclean (Leviticus 15:19-30). Menstruating women were most definitely

Read Leviticus 15:19-30. What insights does this Scripture offer to you about the woman's plight?

not to be out in public. The woman was committing a big taboo just being in the crowd. And yet, there she was, struggling with the rest of the people just to get close to Jesus.

Remember the story of the good Samaritan (Luke 10:30-34)? We are sometimes hard on the priest and the Levite in this story because they passed an obviously injured person and did not stop to help. But if they had touched a seriously injured, bloody person, or worse yet, a dead person, they would have had to withdraw from normal life until they could go through all of the ritual purification rites. To stop and help this man would have delayed them for days. They would not have been able to take part in their religious duties. Ritual uncleanness had serious consequences.

For 12 years, this woman had been isolated from her community and from worship in the temple because of her malady. Like the Gerasene demoniac in Luke 8:26-39, she would have lived outside social boundaries.[1] She suffered not only from her illness but from social isolation as well. Now we are getting the picture. To be ritually unclean meant that she was cut off from normal life—both because she herself was ritually unclean and because anyone she touched would become ritually unclean as well. She was, in effect, "cut off" from her community because of her illness.

The woman in our story was sick with a very debilitating and isolating illness. That is a strike against her. And, of course, she was a woman. Women were not considered fully human in the days of Jesus. They were usually considered the "property" of their husbands, or fathers, or sons. A second strike. She was also poor because she had spent all of her money on doctors. Mark's account of this story places more emphasis on her efforts to be cured by doctors. "She had endured much under many physicians, and had spent all that she had; and she was no better, but rather grew worse" (5:26). Her poverty was

Read Mark 5:21-34. Compare and contrast this Scripture to Luke 8:40-48. What new insights do you gain from reading the story in both Mark and Luke?

Make a list of things that "cut us off" from our community and do not allow us to participate in "normal" life. Suggestions would include chemotherapy, mental illness, poverty, lack of affordable transportation. What examples can you think of from your own experience?

not due to a lack of financial planning. She had spent all that she had hoping to be able to re-enter her society, hoping to regain a "normal" life, all to no avail.

Her poverty, as well as her illness, placed her outside social boundaries. This is a third strike against her.

Even though she is not named in Scripture, we have no reason to believe that she was anonymous. In the twenty-first century, we are often surrounded by strangers. But in the first century, a poor, sick woman would not have gone far from her home. Most likely, everyone in that crowd knew perfectly well who that woman was—including the fact that she was ritually unclean.

So this woman was a very unimportant and powerless woman. But did she act like it? No way! This woman was BOLD. It took guts for her to go out in public. She defied social customs and religious laws and went after what it was that she knew she needed to be whole.

Imagine yourself as one of the characters in this scene. With which character do you identify most? How does your point of view affect the way you hear this story?

Again, Mark's Gospel says a bit more that helps us relate to her desperate and bold hope for healing: "She had heard about Jesus, and came up behind him in the crowd and touched his cloak, for she said, 'If I but touch his clothes, I will be made well'" (5:27-28). When we remember that touching Jesus would have made him then ritually unclean, we get a deeper sense of her boldness. There is something ironic about the fact that for her to touch anyone's clothing would make them unclean; and yet, touching Jesus' garments made the woman instantly clean and whole. She was healed. She was made clean. She knew it, and Jesus knew it. He told her, "Daughter, your faith has made you well; go in peace" (Luke 8:48).

What faith! What boldness! She knew what she needed, and she knew how to get it. But she didn't let social custom, or religious law, or even the opinions of her community get in the way of getting what she needed. She reached out in boldness and got what she needed to be whole.

Remember the young girl Jesus was on his way to heal? During Jesus' encounter with the woman with the issue of blood, Jairus's daughter died. Jesus' words about faith flow into the story. Upon word of the daughter's death, Jesus says, "Do not fear. Only believe, and she will be saved" (Luke 8:50). Once again, we have a healing story that involves ritual uncleanness and restoration. Jesus, even though he would be ritually unclean by touching a dead person, took the dead girl's hand, told her to get up; and she did. She was restored to life. In one sense, the Gerasene demoniac and the woman with the flow of blood were also restored to life. In all three stories, Jesus shatters social and religious boundaries to heal and save people who are in need.

> Read all three accounts of healing in Luke 8:26-56. What similarities do you see in the stories? What do they say about Jesus? What do they say about boldness? What do they say about the power of God?

Exploring the Depths

So what does this story mean to us? Are we to ignore social custom or religious law if there is something we want? Does it matter what anyone else thinks as long as we can get our own way? Are the needs of the community unimportant when they interfere with the desires of the individual? No, these would be surface interpretations. We want to go deeper.

Most of the time, Jesus was asked for healing. And there seems to be a sense that Jesus could withhold that healing if he wanted to. He argues with the Syrophoenician woman about the appropriateness of healing her daughter because she was a Gentile (Mark 7:24-30). Healing often seemed to need Jesus' intention in order to be accomplished. Jesus said things like, "Rise up, take up your mat," or "Your sins are forgiven," or some other phrase of command before the healing took place. But not with this woman. She did not ask—at least not verbally. Jesus did not say anything to her before her healing. Jesus did not *intend* to heal her. And yet she was healed. Did the woman heal herself? No, Jesus felt the power go out of him. Jesus definitely *did* the healing, just not intentionally.

But did Jesus want to heal her? We have no reason to believe that he did not. In fact, it seems pretty clear from reading the Gospel accounts that Jesus wants everyone to be healed of what ails them. The woman knew that the healing of her illness was what she needed in order to be whole. She believed with her whole heart that all she had to do was to touch the hem of Jesus' garment in order to get the healing she needed. So she went for it. She didn't wait for the healing to come to her—she reached out and got it. Her faith made her well.

When we look at our lives and at the lives of those around us, we see many opportunities for healing and wholeness, for restoration and new life. Think beyond physical illness for a moment. Cultures, governments, communities, businesses, families, and relationships all need healing. We can learn from the woman with the flow of blood. We can ask how our own boldness can make a difference.

Diving In

What is it we need to be whole? Do we need healing from chronic depression? Do we need to be able to accept ourselves as we are, rather than comparing ourselves to others? Do we dare go after what we need, with boldness? If a poor, sick, woman had the courage to reach out and touch Jesus in order to be healed, can we work up the courage to reach out for what we need?

Take a few minutes and reflect on these questions to the right. Write a journal entry or draw a picture about your answers to these questions. Find a partner and talk about your reflections with one another.

What would it take to boldly offer or receive God's healing power? We can't wait for someone to invite us to come receive or to give a blessing. We can't sit back and say, "If only life were different, I would be whole." Or "My actions won't matter. I can't do anything to help." We would all love to play the "if only" game: If only my mother had loved me more. If only my child had not gotten sick. If only I had as much money as my neigh- bor seems to have. If only I had married the right person the first

> What are the "if only" messages you have heard? How can playing "if only" stop you from getting what you need?

time. If only I could have had kids later in life. If only that tragedy had not happened to me. If only I had a better boss. If only I had been put in charge of that project. Or on a larger scale, if only there were no poverty. If only nations could live in peace. If only all corporations were honest. If only, if only, if only.

The "if only" game can be fun and certainly relieving. As long as we can blame outside circumstances for our misfortunes and the misfortunes of others, we don't have to accept any real responsibility. But playing this game does not move us toward healing. Most of the time, as individuals, we already have what we need to become whole. Sometimes all we need is an accept- ance of our own limitations. While I could say, "If only I could play professional tennis, like my friend," it doesn't change the fact that I do not have the genetic makeup or physical capability of playing tennis. I can come up with lots of great ideas for making money, but I do not have the business acumen to make my ideas into a money-making proposition. So, if I believe that what I need to be whole is to make lots of money, I am probably out of luck. I spent a good deal of time in my life trying to obtain more money. I would go after the better job, take on additional jobs, and work myself into the ground trying to get enough to make me happy. But it was never enough. Fortunately, I have done enough work in Bible study and prayer and meditation (and therapy!) to know that I don't need lots of money to be whole. In fact, for me, money can be a barrier to being whole. I just need a roof over my head, food in the cabinet, friends and family to surround me, and an outlet for my creative talents to be whole. And lo and behold, I have all of those, in abundance. I came to a point where I was given a choice: I could continue on my career path of more money, recognition, and power (and be miserable); or I could reach out in boldness and take a job with much less pay but much more fulfillment in the end. My choice looked foolish to everyone around me—even to my friends and loved ones. Who takes a major pay cut when they are only ten years from retirement? Most folks thought I was pretty crazy, but I knew what I needed and I reached out and got it. We have to determine what we truly need and then go for it. God wants us to be whole human beings.

> Spend some time reflecting on your path in life. Are you doing the "expected" thing, even when it does not bring you fulfillment? Are you doing more to please others than to fulfill what you truly believe to be your calling?

Now let's be clear. There are circumstances in our lives that cannot be changed. No amount of reaching out is going to bring our loved one back to life. We cannot change our genetic makeup so that we no longer suffer from diabetes, or heart problems, or obesity. Faith does not stop accidents from happening. But what we can do is change our response to the circumstances in our lives. And such change requires boldness.

One of the most profound faith lessons I ever learned was from a young man I will call Jason. Because of a bad reaction to a medication, he will always function on the level of an infant. When he was first diagnosed, we all prayed fervently that somehow he would be healed—that he would be able to live a normal life. One day, it occurred to me that he was living a normal life—for him. Those of us who loved him were the ones who were living the "abnormal" life, from his point of view. Once we were able to accept that normal life meant including a precious child of God who could not stand, walk, or communicate in clear English, we were able to enjoy the wonderful boy that he was. Life has always been hard for Jason's family, but how much richer it has been for those of us who have been privileged to be around him and love him.

Sometimes boldness means reaching out beyond our own needs, as Jesus did, in order to offer God's healing and help. It may mean taking risks and reaching across boundaries to do so. Have you ever participated in a mission trip through your local church? Have you ever considered being a big brother or a big sister to a child? Have you thought about how you might get involved in legislation that would get at the root causes of poverty

> What do you see in your life, in your family, in your community, or in the world that needs healing, wholeness, and restoration? What would it take for true "healing" to occur? How might your boldness make a difference?

or homelessness? What about environmental issues? In every case, our bold action makes a difference, even if the boldness seems to be no more than touching the hem of Jesus' clothes.

So are you ready to dive in? Take a deep breath. Identify the needs. And then reach out in boldness. God's power will be there.

Closing Worship

Gather together around your worship area.

Sing "Lord, I Want to Be a Christian," "O Love That Wilt Not Let Me Go," "Take My Life, and Let It Be Consecrated," "Where He Leads Me," or another hymn of commitment.

Spend some time in silence reflecting on God's call to be bold.

Lay out on a table several random pictures that you have cut from magazines. Include pictures of people, flowers, buildings, children, household objects, and nature. Make sure you have at least twice the number of pictures that you have participants. Ask the participants to choose a picture that reminds them of a situation in which they need boldness. If they feel "bold" enough, allow them to share their picture and what it means to them. Invite them to take the picture home with them as a reminder that God is with them.

Pray: "O God, we know that you want us to be healthy and whole. And we know that you have already given us the tools that we need to achieve wholeness and to offer wholeness to others. Help us to use the courage we have to reach out so that we, others, and our world might be healed and fully alive. Amen."

INTERGENERATIONAL ACTIVITIES

Continue a Work Project

Read the instructions for the work project in Session One. This week, continue to assemble the "sack lunches." Have participants decorate paper bags, write notes of support to include in the lunches, and then stuff them with one of each of the items you have collected. If anyone from your church has distributed any of your lunches, write an article for your church's website or newsletter about your project. Be sure to include pictures of your group assembling the lunches and a description of where they are distributed.

Play a Game

Practice being bold by playing "Shuffle Your Buns." Have everyone in your group gather in a circle of chairs. Make the circle as tight as you can. The person whose name has the most letters gets to be the Bold One (or "It"). The Bold One stands in the center of the circle. The object of the game is to prevent the Bold One from sitting on your immediate left. When a chair becomes empty to your left, scoot into it, leaving a space on your right. This means the person on your right will also have to scoot to keep the Bold One from sitting down. To spice it up, the Bold One can call "Switch!" which means that now the object of the game is to keep the Bold One from sitting on your *right*.

Write a Hymn

Read the instructions for writing a hymn in Session One. Write a new verse about the woman whom Jesus healed. Make sure there is something in your stanza about being bold to help participants remember the purpose of this lesson.

Make a Banner

Tape a large sheet of bulletin board paper to the wall. Have someone draw a figure of a woman standing beside Jesus, and write "Be Bold" in balloon letters across the top of the sheet. Read the instructions for "coloring" this picture in Session One. Place this new picture next to the other pictures. Leave room for one more picture for the next and final session. You are creating a whole wall of pictures to help participants remember the key points of the Bible stories and the purpose of each lesson.

---

[1] See *The New Interpreter's Study Bible* (Abingdon Press, 2003); page 1869.

Diving Into Belief

Focus: Questions about God prepare us for spiritual growth and deeper faith. Believing and experiencing for ourselves brings about a deeper relationship with God and others.

Gathering

Create a worship center by placing a candle and an open Bible on a small table. Print the word "Believe" on blue paper and trim the edges to look like a wave of water. Add to your wall display or your bulletin board.

Light the candle and read John 20:29b. Divide the group into twos or threes and discuss the verse. What does it mean to believe without seeing? After a few minutes, invite the participants to share some of the highlights of their discussion.

Pray together: "Holy God, we live in a world that calls us to believe what we are told. But we are also told to 'read the fine print' and 'ask questions' to keep from being scammed. Help us recognize the tools we need to put our faith in you. Amen."

On the Surface

Can you imagine being a disciple, especially during the crucifixion and resurrection of Jesus? We have heard the story so many times that it is really difficult to grasp the enormity of the experience. The disciples had been following a charismatic leader they believed to be the Messiah, the anointed one of God, who would establish God's realm and who was pointing them toward a new way of being in the world. I can imagine they were just soaking up the experience of being with Jesus and looking forward to the hope of God's kingdom. They had all been there to see Jesus welcomed into Jerusalem with palm branches and shouts of "Hosanna!" (John 12:12-13).

Less than one week after the dramatic entrance into Jerusalem, their world was turned upside down. Their beloved leader had been arrested, tried, and sentenced to death. According to all reports, he had not even tried to defend himself. He was humiliated, beaten, and crucified. This great teacher, whom they had all seen raise the dead and walk on water, would not stop an angry crowd, jealous religious leaders, or the Roman government from putting him to death.

Remember where you were on September 11, 2001? Of course you do. Most of us watched in horror as the Twin Towers suddenly collapsed in on themselves. We heard the reports of an airplane hitting the Pentagon. We heard rumors that there was another airplane somewhere in Pennsylvania that somehow had something to do with another attack. All planes were suddenly grounded. Folks were stranded in far-off cities with no way to get home. Life as we knew it virtually stopped for the day. We were all asking questions, "What is happening?" "Who is attacking us?" "How could something like this happen?" And life has never been quite the same since the horrific events of that day. This would have been the experience of the disciples on that awful weekend when Christ was crucified. They had been following Jesus for months or years and had caught a vision of what life could be like in the realm of God, where women, lepers, and even foreigners were welcomed. They had seen healing and forgiveness. What would they do now? Where could they turn? Were they in danger as well? Could they be the next ones on the cross?

We do not know how many of the disciples were there to witness the Crucifixion. Mark 15:40-41 says that women, including Mary Magdalene; Mary, the mother of James and Jesus; and Salome, who had followed him to Jerusalem, were looking on from a distance. Luke 23:27 also mentions women and other followers. John 19:25-26 says that Jesus' mother; Mary, the wife of Clopas; Mary Magdalene; and a male disciple were close enough for Jesus to converse with them. While we do not know from the Gospel accounts how many and who among the disciples may have witnessed the Crucifixion, they all knew what had happened to Jesus.

We all handle grief and fear in different ways. Many of us need to gather with friends and family to process. Others need to be alone. The same happened to the disciples. Even though Mary Magdalene announced to the disciples that she had seen the Lord, John 20:19 says that they met behind closed and locked doors out of fear. Apparently, they did not believe her. It was in this place of fear that Jesus appeared among the disciples and said to them, "Peace be with you." He showed them his hands and side, and the Scripture tells us "the disciples rejoiced when they saw the Lord" (verse 20b). Then he breathed on them with a breath of life and told them to receive the Holy Spirit (verse 22). This act of breathing evokes images of God's breath of life in Genesis 2:7. Jesus gave this fearful, locked-in group of disciples what they needed to believe. And he gave them what they needed to do God's work (verses 19-23). Try to imagine the tumultuous feelings that the disciples experienced. The events between Jesus' entry into Jerusalem and the Crucifixion must have strained the disciples belief, but the Resurrection and the appearance of Jesus at a time of fear and grief was totally unexpected. The disciples could hardly believe their eyes; but when Jesus showed them the wounds in his hands and side, they realized that even though Jesus had been crucified, he was alive again! Not only was he alive, he empowered them.

> Read John 20:19-25. Imagine that you are one of the disciples present when Jesus appeared. Would it have been easy or difficult for you to believe that Jesus was raised from the dead? What would you have wanted to say to others about the experience?

John 20:24 tells readers that Thomas was not present with the disciples when Jesus appeared to them. We do not know why. What we have is the disciples' report to Thomas and his response to the news that the disciples gave him. In words that echo the words of Mary Magdalene in verse 18, they told Thomas, "We have seen the Lord." Thomas responded, "Unless I see the mark of the nails in his hands, and put my finger in the mark of the nails and my hand in his side, I will not believe" (verse 25). His response was not very different from the disciples' original response to Mary Magdalene's announcement. The disciples locked themselves inside out of fear of indicating their lack of belief. Their belief came as a result of Jesus' appearance.

A week later, Jesus showed up again in the same place. The disciples were together, and this time Thomas was present. Once again, Jesus said, "Peace be with you" (John 20:26). He offered Thomas the same experience that the other disciples had—the chance to touch the wounds in his hands and side: "Put your finger here and see my hands. Reach out your hand and put it in my side. Do not doubt but believe" (verse 27). Jesus' words are more an encouragement to believe than a criticism of doubt and skepticism. The Greek word that is translated "doubt" is *apistos*. A more literal translation of the Greek is "unbelieve." The Greek word translated as "believe" is *pistos*. In essence, Jesus told Thomas to move from unbelief to belief.[1] Not only did he advise Thomas to make this movement into belief, he gave Thomas what he needed in order to make the movement. He had done the same for the other disciples earlier.

> Read John 20:26-27. How do you respond to this description of the appearance of Jesus? What would you have done if you had been Thomas?

Often, when we hear this story we focus on what Jesus said next, "Blessed are those who have not seen and yet have come to believe" (John 20:29b). We think that Jesus is chiding Thomas for needing physical proof in order to believe. But if that were true, why did he appear in the same place a second time? It is as if Jesus came back solely because he knew what Thomas needed that in order to believe. Jesus gave Thomas what he needed in order to believe. And what did Thomas come to believe? That Jesus was, in fact, God. Jesus' appearance prompts Thomas to exclaim, "My Lord and my God!" (verse 28). This remarkable proclamation reveals the identity of Jesus and echoes the opening of John's Gospel. Notice that the very beginning of this Gospel begins with the affirmation that the Word (or Jesus) was God. "In the beginning was the Word, and the Word was with God, and the Word was God" (1:1). And here at the end of the Gospel we see the same affirmation. Many scholars think that the end of chapter 20 was the original ending of this Gospel and that chapter 21 was added later.[2] They believe that the original ending of this Gospel was John 20:31: "But these are written so that you may come to believe that Jesus is the Messiah, the Son of God, and through believing you may have life in his name."

Let's look at this story again. Remember the circumstances. Thomas's world had been rocked to its foundations. Thomas was not afraid of death, nor could he have been too surprised that the religious leaders would put Jesus to death. In John 11, when Jesus contemplated returning to Judea, the disciples warned him that if he went there, he would be in danger. But Thomas said, "Let us also go, that we may die with him" (verse 16). Thomas believed in Jesus—so much so that he was ready to die with him. But nothing in his experience had prepared him for Jesus' resurrection. Once he realized that Jesus truly had been raised from the dead, he believed that Jesus was not only the Son of God, but the living, breathing, presence of God on earth.

Think back to when you first came to believe as a Christian. What did it take to convince you that Jesus was the Son of God? Did you believe because your parents believed? Did you believe because your Sunday school teacher told you to? Did you come to faith after a struggle? If you have not yet come to a place of belief or if you continue to struggle with believing, what do you think would make a difference for you? What do you think Jesus might say to you today? Share your thoughts with one other person.

Exploring the Depths

In John 11, Thomas was willing to follow Jesus anywhere, even to death. But after the Resurrection, Thomas became not only a follower, but a true believer. And he became a believer because of his own experience with the resurrected Christ—not because others had told him of their experiences.

Teachers of children can tell us that there are lots of "tricks of the trade." Want to get a group of 20 preschoolers to stop running around and focus? Start to sing a song. Want to get a classroom of older elementary children to quiet down? Start to whisper. These and other tips are shared among teachers every day.

But any good teacher will also tell you that no one technique will work with every child. Each child is different. Even identical twins may have had different experiences that have shaped their understanding of the world and may need different approaches to learn something. Each of us is a uniquely created individual. I have no idea why God chose to make us so unique. It seems to me that the world would run so much more efficiently if everyone were more alike or if you could at least place people into a few broad categories. Creative thinkers, gather in one place. Bean counters, go to another place. But the world is not like that. We are all a mix of different abilities and different approaches to life. Brain research is showing us that no two brains are wired exactly the same. The exact same stimuli will conjure up completely different experiences in different people.

Soak cotton balls in different kinds of smelly liquid, such as lemon juice, rubbing alcohol, gasoline, baby oil, and strong coffee. Place each cotton ball in its own small resealable container, such as a film canister or small snack container. Invite the members of the group to take a container and open it while sniffing the contents. What memories do the smells elicit? While there may be some similarities in the memories, you may be surprised at the wide variety of experiences in your group.

The same is true for our faith walk. How do we move from being followers to being believers? For some, our experiences as children in a church community are foundational to our belief. Did our Sunday school teachers teach us about a God of love or a God of judgment? (Most likely it was a combination of the two.) Were our parents religious people, and did we have a good experience being raised by them? Did you learn Bible stories as a child, and did you memorize Bible verses? As we grow, our powers of reasoning grow. We are less likely to believe something because an authority figure tells us to believe it. If we respect that authority

> Find a partner. Discuss your journeys of faith with one another. How are they similar? How are they different?

figure, we will give it more weight; but our own experiences will inform our decisions on certain matters. Our powers of logical thinking also grow. We recognize when things we have been taught no longer connect to our experience.

So how do we move from being a follower of Christian teachings to a true believer that the risen Christ is God in the flesh? Differently, of course. One person's journey is never exactly the same as another person's journey. There may be some similarities: summer camp, pastors, the death of a loved one, the birth of a child; but each person will have his or her own unique walk with God.

It may well be that life events make it difficult to move into belief. Catastrophic

> What challenges your journey into deep belief and faith?

illness, financial hardship, broken marriages, abusive relationships, war, and injustice are some examples of life situations that make us question God. How can we believe in the power of the risen Christ as God in the flesh when we experience or witness such things?

The story of Thomas demonstrates good news. In all our journeys of faith, on the road from following to believing, God is with each and every one of us. God in Jesus Christ met the disciples and Thomas in their unbelieving and gave them what they needed in order to believe. God is willing to meet us where we are and give us what we need in order to become a faith-filled disciple.

Diving In

So let's continue to discover God's presence as we continue on our faith path. Notice that I did not say, "Let's get started." We have already started. We just have to keep going.

When I was younger, I truly believed that there could be a moment—or an instance—when I could convert from being a follower to being a believer. Before this date, I was a mere follower. After this date, I would be a firm believer. The truth is, there is never a single moment, only steps. And each step is totally life changing. To grow into becoming a believer is a life-long process that does not end until death. Every day, every moment presents us with new opportunities to believe or to turn from belief. It is up to us to decide.

First we have to trust that God is indeed with us. We do not have the luxury of being able to touch Jesus' hands and side, nor is that necessarily what we would need in order to believe. But we do have to trust. We can recognize God's presence in the nature that is all around us; in the friends and loved ones who walk with us; and in our Bible reading, hymn singing, and corporate worship experiences.

One way to nurture your capacity for trust is to end every day with a reflection on moments when you felt God's presence in your life. We all have them, but we don't always recognize them. Simply naming these instances daily will help us to recognize them more and more. Perhaps a young child came up, unasked, and gave us a hug. Perhaps we smiled at a person on the street, and when they smiled back, we could see the love of God in their face. Perhaps the view from a mountaintop reminded you of the awesome power and majesty of God's world. As we look for these times when God is with us, our faith and trust will grow and prepare us to dive deeper into God's will for our lives.

Find a partner. Talk together about some of the instances in your life that have helped you know that God is with you. If you feel comfortable, share some of the highlights of your conversation with the entire group.

Next we have to question. This seems to be odd advice, when I have just talked about the need to trust and to have faith. But questioning is not the same as lacking faith. Indeed, questioning helps our faith to grow. Children have unquestioning faith. But when we become adults, we are called to question. When we question our faith, it is often strengthened. In fact, our skepticism may be the place where we encounter deep faith.

As we explored earlier, we have all had events in our lives that have caused us to question our faith. Why did the young teacher at the school develop cancer? How could God allow such poverty in the world? To stifle such questions because they are not "faithful" keeps us at a shallow level of faith. But to wrestle with these questions—particularly when we wrestle with them in a community of faith—can bring us to a deeper and deeper level of belief in God.

Share with at least one other person in your group an event that has caused you to question God. How did you handle your skepticism? What learnings did you come up with in your struggle? How was God present for you in your struggle?

Remember always that God is with you and wants the best for you. God has only your best interests at heart. God will meet you where you are and in the ways you need to help your faith to grow. And God welcomes your questions and doubts. So trust, question, and believe!

Closing Worship

Gather together around your worship area.

Sing "Lord, I Want to Be a Christian," "O Love That Wilt Not Let Me Go," "Take My Life, and Let It Be Consecrated," "Where He Leads Me," or another hymn of commitment.

Have participants turn to John 1:1-18. Invite someone to read the passage aloud. Reflect in silence for a few moments. Then ask participants to choose one phrase from the passage that they truly believe. Have them read the phrase aloud. After each person has read their phrase, have the rest of the group respond, "Lord, I believe, help my unbelief," "This I believe," or another phrase of response. When everyone has had a chance to share, close in prayer.

Pray: "O God, believing that we are blessed children of yours—perfect just the way we are—is really hard. So is believing that we can be obedient, kind, forgiving, and bold. Help us to believe in you, in others, and in ourselves. Amen."

INTERGENERATIONAL ACTIVITIES

Write a Poem

Write an acrostic poem. Write the word "Believe" down the side of a large piece of paper. Then think of things that you can believe that begin with each letter in the word "Believe." For example, "Beauty is only skin deep," "Every person is a child of God," etc.

Complete a Work Project

Read the instructions for the work project in Session One. Finish up all of the sack lunches that you have started and plan to distribute them. Write a final report for your church, including instructions on how families within your church could continue the project on their own. Share stories of how it feels to distribute food to hungry people.

Play a Game

Play "I Doubt It." Have each person write down four "facts" about themselves. Three of the "facts" should be true, and one should be false. Try to have the "facts" all sound as plausible as possible, so that it is hard to tell which one is false. Have each person read their facts and the rest of the group should determine which "fact" is untrue. This is a wonderful way of learning some little-known facts about other members of your group.

Write a Hymn

Read the instructions for writing a hymn in Session One. Write a new verse about Thomas. Make sure there is something in your stanza about believing to help participants remember the purpose of this lesson.

Make a Banner

Tape a large sheet of bulletin board paper to the wall. Have someone draw a figure of Jesus and Thomas standing together, and write "Believe" in balloon letters across the top of the sheet. Read the instructions for "coloring" this picture in Session One. Remember to use bright red tissue for the wounds in Jesus' hands and side. Place this new picture next to the other pictures you have created. If needed, "touch up" some of the earlier pictures. Plan to display your wall of pictures to help participants remember the key points of the Bible stories and the purpose of each lesson.

---

[1] See *The New Interpreter's Bible,* Vol. 9 (Abingdon Press, 1995); pages 849–50.
[2] See *The New Interpreter's Bible,* Vol. 9; page 850.